MW00443702

Mining the Bright Birds

Mining the Bright Birds

Poems of Longing for Home

JODY L. COLLINS

Jody Collins
Psalms
104:12

RESOURCE *Publications* · Eugene, Oregon

MINING THE BRIGHT BIRDS
Poems of Longing for Home

Resource Publications
An Imprint of Wipf and Stock Publishers
199 W. 8th Ave., Suite 3
Eugene, OR 97401

www.wipfandstock.com

PAPERBACK ISBN: 978-1-6667-8294-3
HARDCOVER ISBN: 978-1-6667-8295-0
EBOOK ISBN: 978-1-6667-8296-7

"From the center of our soul, God is calling.
The driving force of our existence
Is our longing to find our way home to Him."

—St. Teresa of Avila

Table of Contents

Introduction

THE THEME OF LONGING for Heaven—my true home—while discovering who I am, runs like an unconscious ribbon through much of my writing. The poems that result from this recorded journey are often anchored in the calendar of Creation—the variation of seasons, the song and call of birds as they change through the year, even the familiar, daily presence of my favorite morning chair. All are tangible reflections, signposts that mark my comings and goings. The way we chart our lives is less a straight line on a calendar of days and more a song cycle moving upward into the future, circles growing closer to each other as we move towards the center, where God is.

The poems in *Mining the Bright Birds* reflect this circular, upward journey, beginning with **Waiting Spaces** that reflect the dark and hidden quiet of the in-between and not-yet of a transforming cocoon. Many of the poems reflect an awareness of being anchored in the dark, like the garden soil before something is born. It is significant to note there are more poems in this section than any other; a good deal of life is spent in waiting spaces.

There are other clues along the journey towards home. In **Tuning**, I attend to sights and sounds, noticing the way birdsong reveals the Holy Spirit's quiet avian messages or the way the light changes. The quotidian appearance of birds at my feeder or on the lawn sparks reflection as well.

The poems in **Seasons** provide another way of marking time, with a return each year to familiar markers mirrored in Creation. Winter, Spring, Summer and Fall the cycle continues, layering the years, marking change through the constancy and rhythm of God's natural world.

The last section, **Wayfinding**, explores the journey towards home, belonging and becoming. What will be my compass? Where am I being drawn? Who has God made me to be? *Mining the Bright Birds* seeks to shine a light on these questions amid personal discoveries and the daily unfolding of life that challenges and changes us all.

Sometimes there is a glimmer that shows the way.

Acknowledgments

THE FOLLOWING POEMS FIRST appeared in *Ekstasis Magazine*, June 2021: "Leave Go," "Freedom's Tune" (as "Silent Chorus"), and "Exodus 13."

The following eight poems first appeared on my website, jodyleecollins.com: "Mining the Bright Birds," "Avian Chorus," "Accompaniment," "I Corinthians 13:1" (as "The Waltzing Cat"), "How to Measure Time," "Dew Change" (as "Weather Change"), "Spring's Verb Says," and "What the Birds Say."

A gracious note of thanks to Jen Grace Stewart, professor, poet and editor extraordinaire, who aptly divined the message woven through these words. To Shemaiah Gonzalez, my first cheerleader, thank you for (virtually) jumping up and down on my behalf. And to KC Ireton, boon companion lo, these many years, in all things written on the heart as well as the page.

AFTER PSALM FORTY-FIVE ONE

He gives us means to write His praises
The breath to carry every thought
To hearts and out again to raise us
Above, mere creatures whom He has wrought.
We alone hold pen and ink,
Brush and pencil paper thin.
No other image bears His likeness
But ours His work to enter in.

Waiting Spaces

LEAVE GO

Float and *fly* are
merely different verbs
for surrender. Like
a lingering Monarch
on milkweed or a
leaf layered on liquid
fountain glass, the
steady breath of a
sure, invisible hand
holds. Like holiness
with wings.

COCOON

I slip on this chosen shelter, hide
within silken walls and wonder—
How long will these layers hold?
Fragile pearlescence surrounds me—
who's to say? My shattered self
is still, waiting.
Gauzy quiet and singular,
barren days envelop
me by the hour. I take pains
with my words, listen more,
defy the urgency of unnecessary
things. Spinning a private
insulation preserves me
heart and mind, a soundless
cushion while my soul heals.

No one can chart a butterfly's
birth. Not really. Skin is shed, the
surprise of color shocks as wings
unfurl, breathing life into deep-
down cells.
Chrysalis—gold. All that remains
when death is past and days
have vanished. New life comes,
unfurls its way into the neverseen.
Eclosion complete,
I raise my wings
and fly.

KINTSUGI

How many daydreams precede
a miracle? A glimpse of possible
revealed in a crack, the sliver of a day
yet to be filled with gold?
Fissured plans are so often
reassembled one fragment
at a time, revealing a final
creation — new, pleasing,
different. A fulfillment,
not of broken promises, but
the promise of healing,
with gold.

THE HEART AND WHAT WE MEAN BY IT

Securely tabled, the body
awaits a scalpel ready to
move in. Sure-handed surgeon,
knowing aorta versus vein,
cavity vis-à-vis chamber,
approaches life-saving
infinitesimally.

He leaves the stories undisturbed,
housed within the heart's memory
as it courses, pulses, blood-red notes
wholly clutched by invisible hands.

Delicate machineries monitor
blood, opaque as merlot, up, out
and back again. A rush of oxygen
sluices the brain, ferries golden
cells to the shore of healing.

Surgeon is pleased, chest
swelling with each
suture, clean as a textbook.
Attendants take note.

Sheltered in sleep, the frail
organ pounds, resounds,
recording days and choruses
as conversations pool and
collect, silent but particular
as autographs, ciphered and
seared on the soul. Cached
messages fuel this body
electric, signaling breath,
as spirit awakens stretching this
muscle of memories cloaked in skin.

* *"delicate machineries"* is a phrase borrowed from
Anne Overstreet

EXODUS 13

We are not fond of the chalky
smudge, non-committal sky
that resists clarity.
We beseech the Heavens
for blue — cobalt perhaps or
robins-egg, a declarative
palette to illumine our
days, secure divine assurance
that our plans will not be foiled.
We long for clear light — glass
to mirror sun's presence,
reflect our daily mysteries,
the uncertainty.
But we cannot dwell forever
in light. Brilliance can blind.
We must have shadow seasons
of in-between, the not-yet
of No Clear Answers, shuttered
trust of, *I am with you.*
The sky speaks this alone, *Find my*
pillar of fire at night, the greeting
of each new day in a cloud.
Half in terror, half in wonder,
we follow, as questions lead the way.

RUMBLE GLORY

Like the assurance of morning songbirds
your Presence comes, Lord, daily moving us
with power not our own towards Your
Kingdom, unbidden like a gift.
We unwrap it in awe and wonder, the
nascent surprise of a new morning
fills us afresh with strength from
that life-giving well—creation's energy
in shades of green, a palette exploding
on the horizon.
Take us by the hand, Lord,
lead us there.

AND MORNING AND EVENING
WERE THE FIRST DAY

I feel so disoriented. —K.Camealy

Oriens — of the East, rising sun's home.
Illuminating hills and homes, he feathers
treetops then vanishes in fog's creeping
swarm. I turn again and again on uneven
ground. Feet lose their footing, all sense
of direction, then remember, *Go where
your gaze leads--your feet will follow.*
I close my eyes and whispers remind Who
will lead me. Handed a telescope, I gaze
to a sky full of stars, leading me home
in the ebony dark.

LESSENED LIGHT

Slatish sky spreads above lace-edged trees,
hides the greeting that is always there.
Illumination pours through changing
strata, a lessened light to brighten my room;
graying rooftops dull the edge of day.

Yesterday's cobalt canvas now obscured,
I remember a singular golden globe against
the heavens of mornings past, deposit
the memory, make mental notes to hold me.
So changed is this view but no less true —
*even when I cannot see it, the sun is always
shining.*

LECTIO DIVINA

Creation written on mirrored
branches bathed in autumnal sun,
jeweled flowers at grassy edge,
ruffled leaves against softly muted sky.
The juncos visit, robins arrive and a gaggle
of chickadees fly towards heaven.
God's glory displayed across the skies
while I scan the lines penned in power,
calmed and quieted by His shimmering word.
I'm reading the world.

WHAT HAD BEEN LOST

This is the day I found my purple gardening gloves.
Not all purple, mind you, but leather on the business side,
lost in the melee of home projects, outdoor-type,
stashed behind the paint cans and spackle,
under the eaves, out of the weather.
Irreplaceable, thank you.

Husband offers a remedy.
"No I can't wear your gloves, they're extra-large.
I want mine; they fit. Like a glove."

This is also the day I found the black
peppercorns — 16 ounce plastic container
from the Big Box store. *(Why do we need all those*
peppercorns? And how did such a vast sum go missing?)
Eyes alert for something else, no thoughts of
looking for my gloves, imagine the silent leap inside
as I laid eyes on what had been lost after all those days.

I leave my prayers in odd places, too.
Gathering dust in hidey-hole corners,
out of sight and out of mind.
Forget to remember where I've laid down
my heavy-laden heart, living with the loss
of unanswered thoughts until I go searching
for something else.
Then the Light strikes and the Spirit
tugs. I reach back in the cobwebs, out of the way
underneath all the noise. And I'm found instead by
Him, stretching out his hands with answers I need
to questions I never knew were there,
where He's been waiting all along.

REARRANGING FURNITURE AS AN ACT OF PRAYER

The sofa—busy tapestry, overstuffed, oversized—is moved
with effort, not elsewhere but out of the way, leaving room to think.
The space now softened by carpeted expanse invites me to pause as I ponder
and exhale into the vastly improved room. Gathering my strength,
we struggle with oaken bookcases that must be kept—all those books!—
just not *here*. So downward they go, hoisted carefully 'round stairway
corners, through doorways and out of sight.

I reflect on rearranging the overfilled room of my heart. Notice
how these four walls reflect a freedom in my soul, a connection
between what has been taken away—unneeded décor, too many
volumes, excess furniture—and the intangible furnishings of my
skin-draped house. Spirit settled, I sense an openness to renewing
like a blank and welcoming canvas.

Godward conversations are thus so, an everlasting surrender
of what must go—*is this really important?*—and what to keep—
I'll sit with this awhile longer, Lord. And in between, waiting in
a wider place to receive answers that will surely come.

STIRRING PETITIONS

Center yourself as marigold yolks
drop over the yellow bowl.
Sift and measure your thoughts as
teaspoons of soda, sugar, salt combine.
Let buttermilk stand souring. Wait
for the buttered, glistening griddle
to sing and sizzle, for songs will not come
from your own heart today.
Whisk flour just enough to mix,
stirring petitions while people are
battered a world away.
Give praise for quiet background piano,
the streaming unseasonal sunshine, calling
you to God's presence here in your silent
kitchen, an altar on the other side
of the world.

INSOMNIAC'S SOUNDTRACK

Rain popcorns through steel
spouts, erratic as fireworks in
July. Midnight messenger *plops!*
house to house while the
background swoosh of traffic
waves in the air.
A truculent dog spells his own
waking as late shift tires splash
through sopping streets.

Somnolence evades me.
A default to the waking process
of writing down my world,
I grasp instead this poem in
the muted globe of an empty
kitchen. Leave words on the
page instead of swimming unmoored
in the dark pools of my mind's
near-morning, quiet at last.

GARDEN PREP

In the quiet dark and underground,
worms occupied with making a way
where there is no way, displace
obstacles one gulp at a time,
their leavings become provision
for what's to come, an unfurling
palette of creation now hidden
soil-deep in the quiet dark.

Tuning

MINING THE BRIGHT BIRDS

I strain towards the future,
eyes focused on the far away
past empty, quiet gray,
looking for a hummingbird
in the snow.
Squint at fine twig lines
sliced across white
over emerald in front
of dormant sienna.
I spy her there, gemstone
stately in her royal stance
among the branches.
The view slows me to the present.

It is no effort, truly, to plow
my way through buried days,
if I but gentle my busy self,
settle and sit, sip and settle,
welcome the daytime darkness,
mining the bright birds.

AVIAN CHORUS

This shady place, shrouded
with the shushing of trees,
cathedral of water-sounds
borne on leaves.
Here is worship in the wind
bending carillon chimes
blowing clouds, leaving blue.

Praises lift in birdsong
echoing, asking
Do you hear Him?
Is He not wonderful,
our Creator God?
I concur and continue to
catch the small cacophony—
an anthem to His presence—
without any words, save those
written within me.

LAWN PARTY

Ebony crows strut in silken hats
and graze, cackling conversations about
early dew-covered offerings seed-wise,
feed-wise.
A heated discussion grows regarding the merits
of stale bread, like so much fireside chatting
complete with brandy and cigars.
They gather and gaggle, regale each other
with a story of early flight plans and feather-
nesting ahead, then they're off with an
avian *Cheerio!* And I gather
crumbs for their next visit come dawn.

ACCOMPANIMENT

Birds, their tones both winged and bright
harmonize from branches out of sight
know their parts, score memorized
flash and zoom before my eyes.
Soprano, alto, second, bass
throaty praises from branchy place
echo, float, reverberate
a pause, then celebrate
mornings' rise first slow and quiet
against dull silence now a riot
each song reveals they know their place
background my day, this hallowed space.

LESSONS

If I was inside, enrobed
in comfort, I'd miss the
rickety *chip, chip, chip*
of the cautious squirrel
feasting on my deck.
Still and safe and sure of
surroundings, I'd never feel this lacy,
lingering, gentle breeze
lilting along the leaves.
I savor the outside moments
then return.

Trailing my eyes over white
walls and picture frames,
echoes from creation's message
still speak. I learn from the
gossamered, billowy
waves of web from an
everyday spider, a dot
in the middle of his
filigreed home. He
clings, sure of his
boundaries, never
doubting for a moment
he's right where
he belongs.

DIALOGUE

A little bird chirped in bravado,
"Your thoughts won't fit
those folks, their focus
is more witness
than wonder."
I sang back to Elle
(my avian companion)
"Ironic. With our sights set
on the same country,
telescopes trained
on the celestial view,
wouldn't they welcome
my words?"
"Jay," she replied, "an astute
observer is what they want,
citing signs of life in this land
at our feet where gray reality
and hard shocks live.
"Your words are too hopeful
for them."
Cocking my feathered head,
I wondered,
Hope-filled-too-much?
How can that be?
Nowhere to go with that dead end.
I have run out of seeds,
pecking and scratching
out this poem instead,
reciting the world in song.

THE MELODY

Casting a furtive glance out the window
to open sky and possibility, I yearn on the hour
for that familiar turn around the corner
a stone's throw away. I will myself to
busyness—baking, a book, broad sunshine
in the yard whispering, *stand still a moment.*
Yet my anxious heart returns, framed by open
curtains and wondering, *are they here?*
Back to my tasks, the daily tidying an attempt
to order chaos, then tugged once more to the
view. I worry desire like an insistent tap, tap, tap,
on the glass for a sight that would bring relief,
quiet my vigilant soul.
I consider, *Is this how it is for our Heavenly Father,*
hope scanning the horizon for our return?
Does He steal way and wonder, *Perhaps today*
my child comes home?
I'm confident it is so. Our ever-returning God
consistent in care, always calling like the morning's
songbirds, a tune He pipes to call us back to Him.

FREEDOM'S TUNE

Dust echoes with his not-voice,
the fingered sentence setting her free.
Onlookers speechless, he bends
again to slice truth in the dirt.
His body unfolds, meets her gaze,
crowd vainly listens behind a wall
of words.
She alone reckons with the lines
of melody at her feet, words to a hymn
only two can sing.
Silent accusers drop their score
and vanish, the day's mirage.
She departs with freedom's tune
pouring crystal notes in her
open heart, walks with the song
for the rest of her days.

I CORINTHIANS 13:1

The waltzing cat silently slinks between
shrubbery, tiptoes from concrete to grass.
The only sound as he slips, a bronze
tag at the neck, announcing his
presence. I follow the fairy-light
noises, eye him as he reaches the fence,
vanishes through to the dark, leafy side.
Larger chimes, upstairs and down,
wave in the wind calling, "Listen!",
landing pleasantly on the ear,
truer sounds than the shrill voices
inside the four walls of home
outside my view.

      ***

I was made for *here and hear*—
tuned to the harmony of Heaven
that calls me to attend.
I turn my head, long for ears shaped
for sound like those of my feline friend,
drawn by the whoosh and rustle
of the kingdom his paws explore.
Wish instead to ring, not with the clang
of this earthbound voice, but
a bit of soft twinkling like wind-
driven chimes belling
me towards Home.

HOW TO MEASURE TIME

I swerved around a swallowtail today,
its *goldblackblue* mosaic translated
across the glass and gone.
Street's curbed outline caught the corner of
my eye as the colorburst startled me to
noticing, awakened me to a sight just past
the neighbors.
A sudden glimpse of canines at their master's
feet—heads anon, ears aperk—then they rose
and trotted on.

What if darting visions, experience, growth
were not an arrow whizzing by in time but
instead layers that land over our lives
like a blanket? What might we make of it,
the mundane atop *daysweeksmonths* of
richness, years folding slowly,
one event or view at a time—
like the memory of a butterfly's sighting—
landing, not leaving, laying the bedrock on
which we build our days.

LITURGY OF THE BIRDS

House finches flit, flit, flit,
hummingbird whirrrrrs
hovering over birdseed an
arm's length away.
Red finch jets elsewhere,
bearing left at the bushes
while chickadee perches,
eyeing the feast.

Crows alight silently on
trees straight ahead,
swooping at breakfast
as they loudly announce the morning.
Waterfall freeway sounds and
the drifting moan of a faraway
train add to the soundtrack.

It's a new day, time and weather
allowing an up close and personal
visit deckside. I'm in between—
a commercial interruption —
before the next task ahead,
refueling my soul's eyes,
drinking in joy for the journey.
Let the birds do all the work
while I observe, teacup in hand
ponder, plan and dream.

DEW CHANGE

Chickadees chatter and chirrup
a cheep, cheep, chick-a-dee-dee!
bullying for position
on the fence post.
Breakfast arguments
translate as, "Hey,
no cuts!" Doesn't matter
there's an over-spilling
feeder — ravenous birds
seem blind with hunger.

It's a change-of-weather
morning; dew rests in places
normally occupied by sunshine.
Old Sol's arc lower in the sky
by several degrees, chair cushions
stashed in case of rain.
A different chill lingers
in the air, reminder of
last-year-this-time, like
an old dream of seasons
before, coming on the
morning of a new awakening.

Seasons

TREE PSALM FOR MOTHERS

virere-to be green

Becoming green—ever active
invisible water dynamic, verdant
current. Like chrysoprase deep in
the earth, it surges, purges soil,
powers its way to liquid emerald
stream, deposits life on the shores
of all it touches—leaves, bark, cells,
a microscopic rebellion.

SPRING'S VERB SAYS

Fireworks have nothing on me,
no man-made show can match
this explosive display.
Shocking green here,
shouting magenta there,
showy white front and center.

No gunpowder could blow
breezes like this
to bristle trees,
to whoosh the wind
across the skies,
no factory fierce enough
to produce this bright beauty.

Spring's verb says
the growing will never stop,
but will flow from a fire
deep in the dark, earth-wise,
shoved to the surface, a
shocking eruption.

Spring's verb comes
from nowhere but Godwhere.
The message proclaims,
Life will always come again.

VIOLET PRIMAVERA

What does Heaven matter
when the depths of sin are afoot?
Skullduggery and lies, shouldn't
 we alert one another,
"Watch out! Beware!" spend our days
pointing, flashlights trained on the
enveloping dark?

Pondering the question as I walk
rain-soaked streets, I notice
order, care, attention,
gracing public spaces, laced
with burgeoning Springtime.
Train my eyes instead on
violet, magenta, shocking yellow
on stems illumined in the promise
of vernal sunshine.

I whisper *thanks* to invisible bringers of
delight, notice the way my eyes and heart
lift towards a truer Kingdom above
to a bluer sky. Vow to use the light I bear
and join the unseen flock with faith eyes,
ambling forward to shine beauty in the dark.

SAFE

Leaves dance and twirl—float
like butterflies from last year's
trees, swirling undertow of wind-
driven currents. A sudden gust
waves barren branches nearly
to the ground.

I'm grounded here, centered
with my coffee on the right side
of the day, beginning my watch.
A view through the translucent
frame allows me transport to
the other side while I linger. The quiet
click-clock at my desk, paper
and pen illuminated by artificial light,
also properly grounded, reminds me:
I am safe and sound. Seen.

ONE MUST

One must gather
a chair, a cushion, a small
setting table, field glasses,
cup of tea, these grand books
like quiet friends
then sit.

One must sit, knees crossed in
cushioned chair anchored in
the too tall grass, eyes to
the hawthorn and bayberry,
waving maple, water-sounding leaves
on air.

One must train the eye, not
strain but rest on beauty-
aleaf and aberry, expecting the
rush and wave of ruby
to hide a robin
or two.

One must, footside, be amazed
at this blazing October day,
flames of foliage an avian
chamber of surprises,
ever changing, never ending
one-of-a kind Autumn.

SUN DAY DENOUEMENT

Dragonfly disappears in front
of the dogwood, the crinkled
yellow fabric of its leaves disguises
his translucent wings. The tufted
fluff of chickadees ruffles in the
wind as they cling to their hidden
perches. Staccato highwire artists,
they defy gravity as I blink and they
vanish. Shrub leaves dance like
tenuous spiders hanging by threads.
The day's a gift, a glorious last gasp
of these waning Autumn hours,
sending light and beauty my way
to capture creation's crown of wonder—
these birds, those trees, this day, God's
best curtain call.

WE DESERVE NOTHING YET RECEIVE EVERYTHING

Winter weather awaits. Wrapped in warmth,
light breezes caress my face here in my
solitary chair while busy nuthatches
leave their seeds to zoom and dart.
Gulls squawk the morning awake.
Gold and peridot tip the season's last
leaves, above them an opening through
impatient, scuttling clouds.
Pungent tea warms while my eyes are
fixed on waning, silvered sun against
the trees, all gift.
All God.

WHAT THE BIRDS SAY

You could say
(and you would be correct)
this mottled, colorless sky
leaves one bereft of brightness
You could say (see above)
the empty, lifeless branches
are dull, dormant gray-brown,
slender swords against said
mottled sky. You could say
(well, you know) there's
little beauty in such poor
adornment, small pleasure
in the drab, drear view.

On the other hand, consider —
this backdrop reveals birds best,
awakens one's eyes to their
blazing joy as they dive into
day, zooming messages
across the sky and voicing
words with their flying song,
faithful, faithful, faithful.

THINGS THAT REMAIN, WINTER

There are always birds, hungry messengers
of God's mercy, present at the feeders
just outside my view. The sky still a showoff,
shape-shifting celestial jellyfish, moving
with the mood of moisture in the Heavens.
Leaves photosynthesize, adorn limbs and
branches, a scrim of green's palette against
gray trunks, slender shrub, fading grass.
And You, everywhere present with Your
creation buried in the invisible
that speaks your name.

TWILIGHT, A SMALL SONNET

Light falls now, weightless illumination
quickens this lifeless tabletop and calls forth
quiet glory, day's end and salvation.
Lost, now revealed, earthbound trappings reflect,
lay animated tho' anchored, pooled in
sun's spotlight streaming magnification.

Words rise, muted silence speaking
at a whisper through glass bathed in umber
leaving night's edge and sleep's invitation,
they stay as invited then tiptoe towards slumber.

Wayfinding

INTRODUCTION TO POETRY

I avoided it as long as I could,
skirted the issue like a wallflower
at my first dance, curious
from afar about such beauty
and grace, wondering at the words.
I felt unequal to the task, conversing
with verse — or worse — writing it.
Why, what if I was wrong?
I hesitated long, delayed
the appointed time of our meeting
like an obligatory trip to the dentist.

When at last we were introduced
(by a mutual friend) my fears dissolved
like sugar in a steaming cup
of tea — surprised by the sweet
welcome (never mind the toothache).
I extended my hand, enticed
by the freedom of words
on the page just so, black on ivory,
a gleaming smile beckoning
me to the dance.
I raised my pen and began.

GRANDKIDS ASKED ME

Complaints are afoot in certain close quarters
that my poems don't rhyme, they're merely imposters.
The grandchildren ask me, "Is that how you write one?
I'm not really sure, Nana, your kind's the right one."
"There're no matching endings, really no reasoning.
It's like eating roast beef without any seasoning.
Tasteless and boring, and lacking all color,
we honestly think that there's nothing duller."
Well fine, I give up, I'll leave free verse behind,
and because I'm your Nana, exceptionally kind,
I've put pencil to paper, all right, I can show 'em
read on my dear lovelies, for here is your poem."

BOOKS LIKE A BOAT

Long ago through pages, my childhood travels
widened the world, weighted vessels carrying me
with words away from the noisy silence of loss
and longing to shores of a new land inhabited
by people cloaked in care and grace.
Pages unfolded, character's lives ferried like
boxed fruit, a cargo of rich phrases
offering a banquet for my soul and instead
of boundaries, welcomed me to the limitless
land of life as it could be.
Would be.
Maybe should be.
I've been voyaging there ever since.

PRODIGAL

Like a bad dream,
footfalls repeat their pattern,
the worn path going nowhere.
Finally, movement.
No actual danger, yet you flee
in the wrong direction, away
from the One who will
bring rest, refreshing, renewing.
You heed instead old lying
voices, snares that keep you
from freedom. Untruths about
another way
this way
any way
but the
Only Way
and all the time He's there.

A whisper, a turn
and you come to the end
of yourself, to His outstretched arms
receiving you, a release
from unnecessary flight;
He declares with joy,
Welcome home.

THE SCARLET SITUATION

—from a phrase by Savannah Locke

Come, family, let us reason together.
When troubles come, and they will,
I've been promised a place to hide,
salvation purchased with my pledge
now honored in return. We'll be
safe from harm here in broad daylight
because of this thread— woven
vermillion skeins taut with promise,
a crimson sign for our enemies to
leave us be in peace, in place.
Their oath that salvation would
rest on ruby draping the window
preserving a seed inside
for generations
who'll come
to be sheltered
once more
in red.

WAYFINDING-ONE

If this world is the book of God,
it spins too fast to linger over
divine language, an oration we
miss, pointing its compass
beyond the horizon.
Alas, I find it's not the needle
that moves, but me—spinning.
A revolving top or door swinging
on its hinges, undone by a breeze.
Now I choose, holding both compass
and view—poised on the day's
threshold. Notice the dawn, read
creation's lines and linger as the
path unfolds.

WAYFINDING-TWO

Mariners charted their course by the stars,
steadfast, sure, fixed, celestial landmarks
guiding the way, constellations like
anchors in the sky.
Turning waves rolled under vast vessels,
threatening to capsize crew and craft
and still they steered, undeterred,
displacing oceans and the immediate
known for horizons filled with the
neverseen.
A fellow mariner, I chart my
course and sail on.

SPYGLASS

Someone is dying soon — pen
in hand in heart, naming
away their end, raising a
glass to the young, sure of
the horizon.
Two become one under
the same sun, dark mystery
beginning in the light where
God will unfold His care
in countless ways as love
leans in, peers forward
into Heaven (on Earth).
The signs are not all that clear.
No manual, "This is How to
Leave your Life."
No promise, "Safe Marriage
Guaranteed."
Still.
A voice calls clearly
through open sky, urging pilgrims
towards the vista where a sure
vessel awaits and faraway
shores are calling them home.
They raise their glass and sail.

STORYTELLER

"You are a storyteller, too. Which stories are serving your life and freedom? Which ones will you keep telling?"
—*Christa Wells*

I am counting words on pages
in the chapters of this book that's my life.
Want to read the ending, long for a sneak
peek at the finish, ignore the slow reveal, the
unwind of line upon line, cover to cover.
My Editor reminds me the pen is not mine
to hold while this story is told. Instead
I offer the blank spaces to Him,
surrender grand ideas and lean
into the love between the lines
as He spells my tale one single letter
at a time, punctuating my days.